'For a time the horse found himself a job pulling a milkman's cart.' The Clothes Horse (1987)

# JANET'S LAST BOOK

*Janet Ahlberg 1944-1994*

*A Memento*

ALLAN AHLBERG

*Consultant Designer* Douglas Martin
*Editor* Christine Collins
*Cover photograph* Glyn William

PENGUIN BOOKS
Published by the Penguin Group
Penguin Books Ltd,
27 Wrights Avenue, London W8 5TZ, England
Penguin Books USA Inc.,
375 Hudson Street, New York, New York 10014, USA
Penguin Books Australia Ltd,
Ringwood, Victoria, Australia
Penguin Books Canada Ltd,
10 Alcorn Avenue, Toronto, Ontario, Canada M4V 3B2
Penguin Books (NZ) Ltd,
182–190 Walrau Road, Auckland 10, New Zealand

Penguin Books Ltd, Registered Offices:
Harmondsworth, Middlesex, England

First published privately by the author 1996
Published in Penguin Books 1997
10 9 8 7 6 5 4 3 2 1

Set in Linotype Diotima
by Goodfellow & Egan, Cambridge
Printed in England by BAS Printers,
Over Wallop, Hampshire

Janet Ahlberg was most widely known as an illustrator of children's books, but there was more to her than that, as you will see – not hear, though, which is a pity. She had a lovely laugh and did excellent chicken impressions; clucks, wings and all.

*Starting School (1988)*

*Bye Bye Baby* (1989)

Contents

*Early Work (c. 1954)*

# THE SCARF

t is September, nine o'clock one morning. I have taken up her breakfast tray: porridge, maple syrup, glass of milk, plus a few other things: Tylex and Voltarol for the pain, Zantac to protect her stomach lining from some of the other drugs, Maxolon and Kytril for sickness after chemotherapy.

The sun comes in at the window. I pull up a chair and sit beside the bed. Janet sips her milk through a straw. She looks at me, mildly – her usual gaze, then past me, over my shoulder to something on the mantelpiece.

'Rose'd like that scarf,' she says.

*The Baby's Catalogue (1982)*

*Janet aged three*

Some people, as their lives go by, acknowledge death, talk of it, let it out and look at it from time to time. Others, the majority perhaps, don't, preferring to stay mum. Jan was one of these. She had been gripped by breast cancer for almost two years. It had spread to her bones and now her liver. Well, she had read the books and BACUP pamphlets, was realistic and knew the score. She had her massive fears and tiny hopes (until the very end), but *said* nothing. Until this day.

'Rose'd like that scarf,' she said.

I knew entirely what she meant. It was her first bequest.

So Jan began to deal with death. Typically, for her, she approached it first with presents. She had a small notebook, a page per person. Often the items were drawn as well as listed. There was, however, no particular system. The whole thing was simply driven by her powerful memory. She just recalled that someone once had expressed a liking for something: '*Byron*: Fish poster in studio', or was present when something else was bought: '*Felicity*: Turquoise shoes with heels and bow'.

Janet dealt with death, faced it, hated it. She didn't want to leave; the party was still going on. There was a manuscript waiting, proofs in the pipeline, a plaintive cat stationed by the fridge and Red Dwarf on the telly. Most of all, of course, there was Jessica (nearly fifteen), her beloved daughter.

*Bye Bye Baby*

11

The days passed. Janet's life was shrunk to a little patch, a few hours in the afternoon downstairs on the chesterfield. A couple of times she spoke of her own funeral. Jan was not religious. She wanted a secular ceremony and burial in the local cemetery. It was her wish that family and friends would gather together, sing a bit and speak for her. She wasn't solemn either. At one point, smiling her slight sly smile, she said, 'Tell Graham he's allowed to say "bum"' (guaranteed with her to get a laugh).

It's February now. Janet has been dead three months. In the bedroom her last-worn clothes hang over the end of the bed, her numerous shoes still clutter the floor and her perfume lingers (mainly because I spray it around from time to time). On the mantelpiece: some talc, some rings, a foolish-looking knitted rabbit and a polystyrene head with a wig on it, bought just in case and luckily (!) not needed. There is a box of bargain jewels . . . but no scarf.

*For Jessica –*
*eve of clarinet exam*

Good luck Jessica

# SOMETHING WORTH HAVING

Special back chair

I love working and listening to the radio. I hate throwing anything away - just in case.

'Do you use pictures (for reference) in your work, or memory?'

'It's not all memory, especially when I know what's in my memory may not be right. If I needed someone in a certain costume, I'd look it up, make sure I had it as right as I could. I'd hate to make a mistake. Recently, I've taken more photographs. When I had to do a book about starting school, I went to Jessica's school and did some drawings, but I also took photographs. I took photographs on our holiday last summer of landscapes that I've since used in *Bye Bye Baby*. I did a bit of drawing as well. But I'm not good at sitting in fields with white paper. If the weather's good enough for you to be sitting there, the paper's bright enough to blind you. If it isn't, it's probably raining.'

'Anything else you'd like to say about your work?'

'Only that we love doing it. But it is a bit strange. The other day we found ourselves having a ludicrous conversation about talking biscuits. It was in connection with a book we're working on. But it's nice that it does end up, we hope, in something worth having.' (Interview published in *Artists of the Page*: Marantz, 1992).

And sometimes the children

 are happy,

and sometimes they are sad;

sometimes puzzled – or sleepy –

or grumpy – or lumpy – or spotty!

*Burglar Bill (1977)*

Janet loved to work. Often in the old days she'd be up until two or three in the morning. She had patience and persistence. In twenty years or so, she produced about fifteen hundred separate pieces of artwork and a mountain of roughs. I've included here a few of my favourites, most of which were hers too.

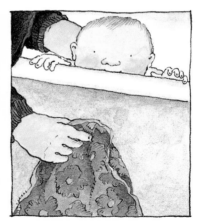

*The Baby's Catalogue*

# MRS WOBBLE THE WAITRESS (1980)

*'The next day the Wobble family turned their house into a café.'*

Janet's early work, in *The Brick Street Boys*, for instance, had a certain stiffness she was keen to get rid of. Her goal, for much of her working life, was to retain the liveliness and spontaneity of her roughs. These roughs were in pencil and often tiny; the finished work was usually drawn with a dip-in pen; the colour, watercolour.

# MR WOBBLE THE WAITER.

The Wobbles run a cafe. Mr Wobble waits, Mrs Wobble cooks, the children wash-up. Mr Wobble is accident prone. Other Happy Families are the customers. The tale follows the ups and downs of one day with a well-earned rest at the end.

The Wobble's cafe-place is charming, food delicious, children clever and hardworking. The only problem is Mr Wobble. Though he is in affectionate regard by all (his customers pull his leg with 'waiter' jokes) he has a tendency to fall

cloths with lace edges and crisp folded napkins

**Mr Wobble**
Gets confused with his orders and serves the wrong things

**Mrs Wobble**

**Master Wobble**
Has delivery boy bike to fetch veg. from market. Buys bread rolls from Mr Bun the Baker.

**Miss Wobble**

Menu is hand written and drawn by Miss Wobble

*An early outline to impress the publisher*

18

*An even earlier rough*

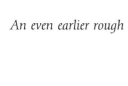

*A full colour sample*

*The final version – Mrs Wobble*
*takes over*

19

## PEEPO! (1981)

'What research did you do for *Peepo!*?'

'I have a wonderful book, the Army and Navy Stores catalogue (1939–40), with beautiful engravings of every conceivable household object – and prices. I get waylaid every time I look in it.' (*Artists of the Page*.)

Janet in her own life threw little away, and often, it seems, made sure her characters didn't either. Incidentally, having invented the mother's dress in *Peepo!*, she subsequently found pretty well the selfsame garment on an old clothes stall in Leicester market (50p).

A word about eyes. In Janet's work, the eye is usually a curiously expressive dot. But for *Peepo!* she experimented, at my request, with a more detailed eye. I had some doubts about the dot in those days. Well, I'm glad about *Peepo!*, but otherwise I was wrong. Jan, in any case, dotted her eyes thereafter.

*The Peepo family –*
*preliminary drawings*

## COVERS

*First rough*

Over the years Janet came up with some good covers; often it was all there in the first rough. Usually, though, she'd press on with alternatives, just in case. On rare occasions, we would disagree – about *Starting School*, for instance. The rule was: if it was words, I prevailed; pictures, she did. So for *Starting School* my choice was shunted to the back cover. Sometimes, of course, the publisher prevailed. The cover for *The Bear Nobody Wanted*, unwanted by Penguin, ended up as the frontispiece, which we regretted. Janet's original cover for *Bye Bye Baby*, thought too solemn by Heinemann, was replaced eventually by something all of us liked. Again Janet's original survived on the back.

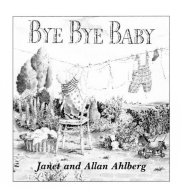

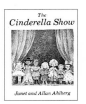

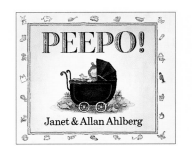

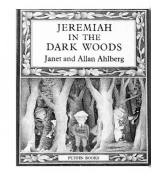

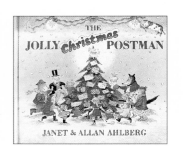

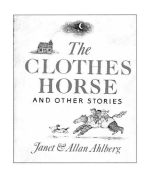

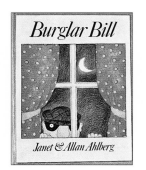

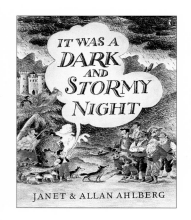

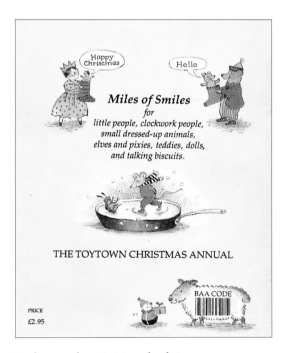

*Back cover for miniature book in
The Jolly Christmas Postman*

*Cover rough (rejected)*

## BYE BYE BABY (1989)

Probably my favourite example of Janet's work. The book, though, had a chequered life. It started out as one of a set (with another illustrator): Robot Baby, Giant Baby, Jelly Baby, etc. Rejected and left in a drawer for three or four years, it somehow got out and onto Janet's board. Afterwards, when the book was published, we spotted a mistake. The baby's beloved toy rabbit was not included in his packing (small suitcase on the half-title and elsewhere). For the paperback edition, Janet painted it in.

*Bye Bye Baby roughs*

*Drawing made on holiday
with Bye Bye Baby in mind*

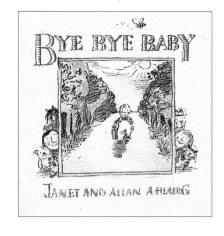

*A couple of unused cover ideas*

*Research – Army and Navy
Stores catalogue (1939–40)*

29

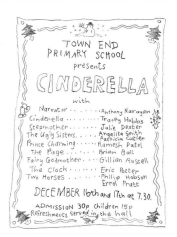

This book also spent some years neglected in a drawer. Eventually, we took the miniature pencil dummy that Janet had made and set out to publish a polished version of that. The scale and medium seemed suddenly appropriate, and in any case the larger full-colour version we'd originally conceived would have taken Janet years. Besides which, other jobs were pushing themselves forward.

*'Snoring softly and dreaming of his childhood days.'*

# BURGLAR BILL (1977)

When we started out, for the first year or two, we submitted work to many publishers and had it rejected. The system was: I'd write something, Jan would do sample pictures and we'd post it off. While awaiting a response, we'd work on something else and send that off, like messages in bottles. At one stage we had four or five packages on the go. After about eighteen months and as many rejections, suddenly in one week Penguin took *The Old Joke Book*, A. & C. Black took *The Vanishment of Thomas Tull*, and Heinemann took *Burglar Bill*.

*Burglar Bill*, I may say, was somewhat bulkier in those days (48 pages) and less inclined to remorse. In our original version he just retired happily ever after to a farm. It took some determined editing to get him to give everything back.

*Unused retirement roughs*

# EACH PEACH PEAR PLUM (1978)

*Each Peach Pear Plum* was the book I most often used to explain publishing to audiences of young children: I do the words (took me about a day) and Janet does the pictures (took her about six months). Then we send the words and the pictures to the publisher and the publisher sends us some money. And I get half the money for my day's work, and Janet gets half for her six months' work (smiles from the teachers): the basis of a happy marriage.

*The cover – roughs and
final version*

_Early rough_

'Mother Hubbard down the cellar
I spy Cinderella.'

# IT WAS A DARK AND STORMY NIGHT (1993)

Janet wanted a grainy effect for her pictures in this book. To achieve it, she enlarged her pencil drawings and worked with coloured pencils (mainly) on the resulting stats. The example (over the page) has been cropped slightly to fit the space.

A postman in a tunnel,
A dog head over heels.
A rabbit in a hurry:
'He moves like he's on wheels!'*
A letter in a rabbit's paw,
A letter on the ground.
A postman with a puzzled look:
'... What's this I've found?'

* He is!

And now - hurray! - the Postman sees
A table set beneath the trees,
A girl (named Alice) in a chair,
A Hatter and a Mad March Hare.
'Goodbye!  Hallo, there!  Lovely weather!'
The Hare and Hatter shout together.
While Alice says, 'Here, sit by me.
How are you?  Would you like some tea?'

The Postman sips, the Postman drinks.
The Postman shivers, smiles ... and <u>shrinks</u>.!
                 What will he do?
                 How will he cope?
                 He's shut up
                 Like a telescope!*

* And his dog, too.

14   15 Envelope front ②

Hatter has book of stamps in
hat band instead of 10/6

Contains a
circular

16 17 18

19
Cakes labelled 'Eat Me'
Tea cups labelled 'Drink Me'

*Part of a complete pencil layout
to astound the publisher*

# THE JOLLY POCKET POSTMAN (1995)

When working, Janet would consider each book in its entirety, the balance and rhythm of words and pictures, pages and spreads; the whole thing, cover to cover. She produced layouts and dummies to show us what we had and ensure that it worked. Her natural scale was small; she was essentially a miniaturist. For this reason, if no other, *The Jolly Pocket Postman* was for her an ideal job: small leaf-size, lots of little pictures – even a magnifying glass. It was a target she could hit.

Meanwhile, a girl
so hugely high
You'd need a *telescope*
to spy
If she had washed
her neck or ears,
Above the 'tiny' trees
appears.*

'It's only me,
for goodness sake;
All I did was eat a
cake.
Then I shot up like
a rocket!'
She has the Hatter
in her pocket.

*Alice, of course

Sequels are a risky business. Better nothing at all than a book that drags its partner down. This sequel owes its existence to a pile of letters from a school in Texas. The children were full of praise for *The Jolly Postman* and *The Jolly Christmas Postman*, and urged us to continue. Why not an Easter Postman, or Hallowe'en, or Valentine's Day? Dorothy (Kansas and Oz), it was suggested, might meet this really cute boy – the Postman, of course – at the junior prom.

Anyway, the letters did the trick. A couple of things fell into place, Jan drew some roughs, even before the text was written, and we were off. Only then did we notice a *teacher's* letter in the pile. This revealed that actually the children had written their letters as part of an assignment to *get* us to do another book: an exercise in persuasion. We gave them ten out of ten.

*The Jolly Postman (1986) – above*
*The Jolly Christmas Postman (1991) – right*
*The Jolly Pocket Postman – facing page*

*The Jolly Postman –*
*pages from Jan's first dummy*
*(actual size), plus final*
*version of tipsy postman*

# A LOVING MEMORY

Minnie
our small cat
who likes buttons,
sinks and going
everywhere.

*Janet and friends –
holiday snap*

Janet kept things. When we were first married, I remember carrying a stack of boxes from her dad's house out to a van. Graham, who was helping me, dropped one. Out spilled half a dozen exercise books: Janet Hall, Form 3A, History. She was twenty-four at the time.

The other day, I opened one of her drawers in the bedroom and a compressed mound of tights came up to meet me like a rising loaf. There were not just masses of tights in that drawer, it seemed to me, there was the *history* of tights.

But it wasn't the contents of boxes or drawers that made Janet special, it was what filled her head. She had a remarkable *loving* memory. She could remember in great detail much of her own life and, more to the point, almost as much of her friends' lives. As she herself wrote, just weeks before she died: 'My dear Rose, We go back a long way – who else remembers your entire 1975 wardrobe!' Who else? Well, probably not even Rose. On the other hand, ask her what she'd earned in 1975, or any other year, and she couldn't tell you.

*Portraits of Minnie – illustrated letter (1990)*

*Portraits of Pinkle –
illustrated letter (c. 1954)*
    *'Dear Mummy and Daddy,
I hope you are both alright.
Thank you for the comics. I
wondered if the new positions of
Pinkle would make you laugh!'*

*Ingrid's box*

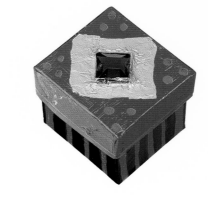

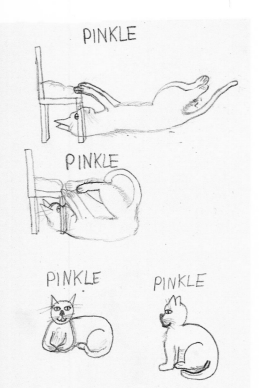

PINKLE

PINKLE

PINKLE    PINKLE

Jan remembered scores of birthdays and her Christmas lists were a sight to see. Her goal was always the *appropriate* gift, and if she could find it on a junk stall, so much the better. She also loved making things and giving them away: boxes, vases, bowls, from card or papier mâché often covered in a patchwork of delicately wrought sweet wrappers. Jessie and I did our bit too, eating the contents.

    *Fairies (1953)*

*Allan's vases*

*John and June's mug*

*Byron's box*

*Family plate*

47

Beano *and* Krazy Kat *birthday cards. Janet, among other things, was a talented forger.*

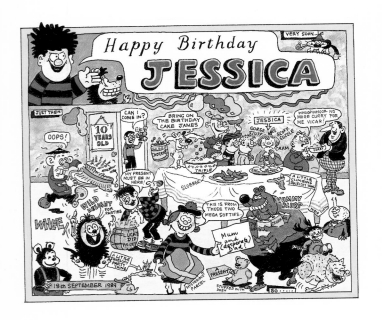

*Happy Birthday Allan - with lots of love from Jan X*

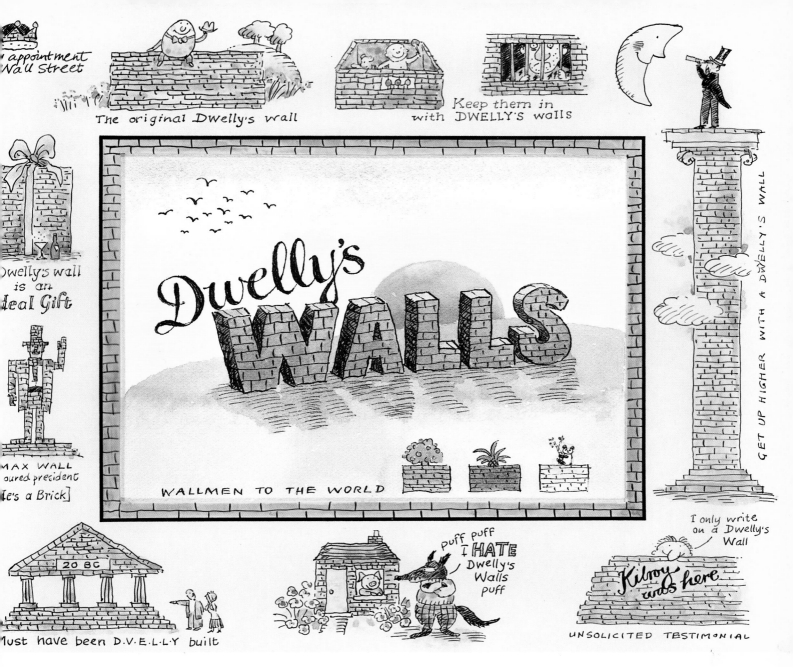

appointment Wall Street

The original Dwelly's wall

Keep them in with DWELLY'S walls

Dwelly's wall is an Ideal Gift

MAX WALL oured president [e's a Brick]

Dwelly's WALLS

WALLMEN TO THE WORLD

GET UP HIGHER WITH A DWELLY'S WALL

Must have been D.V.E.L.L.Y built

PUFF PUFF I HATE Dwelly's Walls puff

I only write on a Dwelly's Wall

Kilroy was here

UNSOLICITED TESTIMONIAL

*When part of our garden wall fell down, a good friend (Colin Dwelly) rebuilt it. Jan showed her appreciation.*

*Peg people – survivors from school fund-raising stall*

After Janet's death, we found a hoard of her last Christmas presents squirrelled away in the studio. Eventually, we matched them to her final uncompleted list – Carol, Victorian plates, tartan notebook; Glyn, Mexican mirror; Katy, Bunnikins bowl – and passed them on.

*Christmas card roughs (1994)*

# UNFINISHED BOOKS

*oh we do like to be beside the seaside*

*Mr Soot the Sweep*

Sharing work with Jan was a particular pleasure. She did the pictures, I did the words, together we made the book; together we *surrounded* the book, played tennis with it. And when one was done, of course, we'd do another. At the end, though, there were books unfinished, quite a few of them.

*'The train arriving at platform two
is crowded with crooks
and a day and a half late!
British Rail apologise for the delay.'*

## HAPPY FAMILIES

Janet did lots of work on the Happy Families series
that never made it into print; Mister Soot the Sweep,
for example. Later on, the last drawings she ever
completed were roughs (too rough, in her opinion)
for other Happy Families stories. These she drew
on her lap in the sitting-room, or at a makeshift
drawing-board in the bay window, half an hour
at a time.

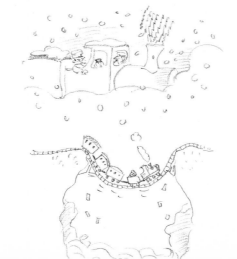

*'He travelled everywhere
with his mum and dad.'*
*Master Track's Train*

'Clara Cliff takes Clifford Clamber to be her lawful wedded husband.'
Ms Cliff the Climber

'No job is too little.
No job is too big.'
Mrs Vole the Vet

No job too tall

too big

Too small

injecting butterfly / ant / beetle

"He's swallowed something"

supposed to be a cup of tea + saucer make recognisable object

Too low

Hmm!

Too spotty (measles)
But is leopard anyway which are spots?

Push off, shut the door Don't come back

Too rude

Too complicated

Too fast

Hamster in wheel can hardly see it

Too wet

Too frightening (putting pill in mouth)

# SAUSAGES!

This was something we'd had around for years. It was an idea for a book that would be full of mistakes. When the reader spotted one he was supposed to yell, 'Sausages!'

This book has twenty three mistakes. When you spot one Shout...

The sausages are here to help you.

— no we're not

sausages?

sausages
school dinners

So the little Red Hen went to talk to the striped cat.

No, no she went to talk to the spotted dog.

Thanks. 'Will you help me to grind the corn?' she asked. 'Not likely' said the dog

Sausages — her riding hood should be yellow

Double sausages — it should be red

little blue riding hood, was frightened she did not want to speak to the wolf.

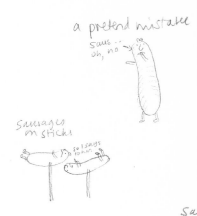

a pretend mistake

saus... oh, no

sausages on sticks

saus...

54

# STRIPS

In this book three stories told in comic strip would become entangled. The regularities of the strip would be overthrown, characters would escape into neighbouring strips, and plots would thicken. Janet's rough, shown here, was produced some years ago when the idea first occurred to us, and before the strips themselves had been worked out.

# BOREDOM

When Jessica was about six, she came into the kitchen
one day with a cardboard thinks bubble lashed to a yardstick
held behind her back and over her head. 'Boredom', it said.
She was trying to tell us something. The message we received,
however, was rather different. 'Hm . . . a *book*.'

57

## THE GASKITTS (A SERIES)

The Gaskitts, had they come off, would have been a set of easy readers with titles like The Man Who Wore All His Clothes, The Woman Who Won Things, and so on. We had in mind a sort of family soap set in a universe where pets could talk and *everything* was animated.

Good morning Mr Gaskitt

59

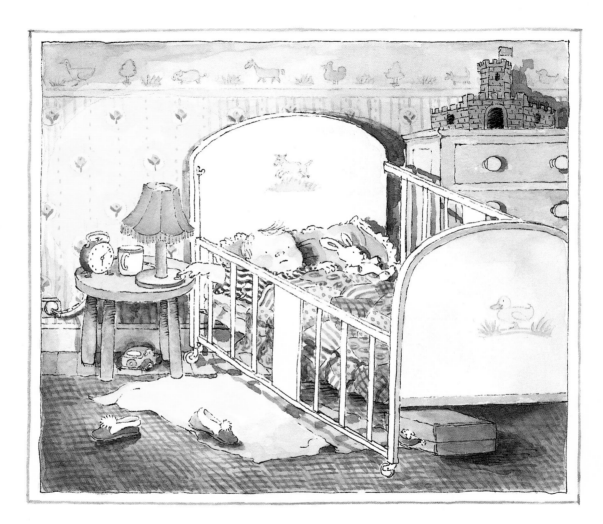

'I need a mummy!'
Bye Bye Baby

# POSTCARDS

In the last weeks of her life Janet was unable to work at all (a real sign she was ill). Instead, what little energy she had was spent in writing farewell postcards to her family and friends.

'It's awful writing goodbyes to my best and oldest friends but I suppose that's what this is . . . I wanted to give you something to remember me by . . . The beaded bag is one that belonged to one of my mother's aunties . . . We go back a long way – who else remembers your entire 1975 wardrobe! . . . I wanted to watch all our girls' progress – it's so fascinating when they've been friends for so long . . . After you were born I counted your fingers and toes for some odd reason – worried that maybe 4/6 fingered gloves/socks might be a problem . . . I've asked Allan and Jess to look out some of my jackets and things for you to remember me by. I'd be so pleased to think you could bear to wear them – don't feel you *have* to, but the green one does suit you! . . . You've made me laugh so much and always lightened life – a totally irreplaceable old friend . . . I don't want to leave but perhaps I'll just go on ahead and put the kettle on . . . Love, Jan.'

*'His trousers were stolen by a couple of tramps.'*
*The Clothes Horse*

# MEET
## Janet Ahlberg

I'm not very keen on having my photograph taken.

How far can a pirate ship go? / 15 miles to the galleon

I was born in Huddersfield on Trafalgar Day 1944.

*An autobiographical piece for the Puffin Magazine (1988)*

When I was little I was brought up with Rupert and Pooh whom I loved.

I now live in Leicestershire and work in a studio above the garage.

Special back chair

I love working and listening to the radio. I hate throwing anything away – just in case.

The members of my family are:

Allan, my husband. He likes reading, writing and playing badminton.

Jessica, my daughter. She likes reading and teddies.

He has only half a tail

Jack, the cat. He likes eating and guarding the fridge.

John, Josie and Dinky Jessica's goldfish.

Our books usually begin with an idea of Allan's...

... for which I do lots of rough drawings and add ideas of my own. I take a long time to illustrate a book – 9 months to a year.

How did Little Bo Peep lose her sheep? / She had a crook with her

What's bad tempered and goes with custard? / Apple grumble

Have you heard about the man who bought a paper shop? / Yes – it blew away

I've illustrated about 40 books for children. The first were about making things from card and empty yogurt pots.

*The Clothes Horse*

Janet disliked hyperbole, the language of blurbs, had trouble with compliments and much preferred the understatement. So what then would she make, I wonder, of what I am about to write?

Janet *was* special. Yes, I know, there are lots of good-hearted people in the world, a fair number of funny ones; there are talented people and people with rich, dense, loving memories. But to possess the set of all these attributes *and* do ace chicken impressions – that's rare.

*The Jolly Christmas Postman*

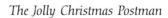

And now it's April. There's talk of turfing Janet's grave, raising a headstone. A commemorative poster is coming out, and the first bound copies of *The Jolly Pocket Postman* have just arrived. In the bedroom Jan's shoes still clutter the floor and her clothes still hang on the end of the bed. It's time I moved them.